Searching for Sea Lions

Kim Westerskov

Learning Media

CONTENTS

CHAPTER 1

Campbell Island is a wild and lonely place. I went there to help make a film and a book about Campbell Island and some of the other islands nearby. I had visited Campbell Island once before, so I had already met many of the animals that lived there – the albatrosses, the penguins, and the seals … and the giant crabs! Most of the time, it's wet, windy, and cold. But it can also be very beautiful.

My usual job is taking photographs of the sea and its animals. I also travel to faraway places like Antarctica. It's a great job. I think it's the best job in the world.

On this trip, I wanted to film Hooker's sea lions swimming underwater. Filming the sea lions on land is no problem, but filming underwater was not going to be easy. Another photographer had tried for days, but the sea lions wouldn't swim near him. I had been swimming with sea lions and fur seals many times, and I was keen to try again.

Every year, thousands of Hooker's sea lions breed on the Auckland Islands, but one or two hundred "pups" are also born each year on Campbell Island. The Hooker's sea lion and the Australian sea lion are the two rarest sea lions in the world.

The Navy took us to Campbell Island on one of their ships. They were going to spend six weeks making new charts of the seas around some islands to the south of New Zealand.

The charts would make it much safer to sail around these islands. Our film crew and a group of scientists "hitched a ride" to Campbell Island.

After three days' sailing, Campbell Island
appeared out of the gloom. It looked dark
and stormy.

CHAPTER 2

Before I go on any trip, I read a lot about where I'm going. I had found these facts about Campbell Island.

Rain days per year:	325
Snow days per year:	42
Hail days per year:	69
Average wind speed:	31 knots (a gale)
Average air temperature:	44 degrees F

We could only stay four days at the island, and then the ship and its crew had to move on to the next island. I knew that I'd be very lucky if I got a good day for my pictures and film.

For the first three days, the weather was bad. Out on the coast, where most of the sea lions lived, it would be too rough for diving. While we waited, I photographed sea lions on the beaches.

11

There are four kinds of seal on Campbell Island – sea lions, fur seals, leopard seals, and the huge elephant seals.

Leopard seals only visit from time to time, and fur seals are usually found on the rough, rocky parts of the coast. But elephant seals are common in the harbor. Elephant seals are the largest of all the seals.

The males can be up to 16 feet long and can weigh over 7000 pounds. They are also champion divers – they can swim down to 4700 feet and can stay underwater for up to 2 hours.

It was fun photographing the elephant seals and sea lions on the beach – but I already had a lot of photographs like that. I needed underwater pictures.

CHAPTER 3

For a lot of the time, my diving buddy needed to be with the film crew. When he had spare time, we took a small boat and went diving. We used torches to look into underwater caves, and we found some giant crabs. One of them snapped my pencil in half with its claws. I kept my fingers away!

When we looked under the large rocks on the seafloor, we were amazed by the rich and colorful life growing there. The seaweed grew in underwater forests that we could swim through. I've always liked the way this seaweed sways and dances in the current.

Finally, on one dive, I found a sea lion underwater – or rather, it found me.

This female gave me a fright – she rushed up behind me, and I didn't see her coming. Sea lions like doing that.

I once met one that made a game out of it. She would swim away in the dirty water until I couldn't see her. Then she would try to sneak up behind me. When I was facing the wrong way, she would rush up and grab hold of my flipper, as if to say "I won!"

But this sea lion didn't want to play games. I only got one photo before she disappeared.

CHAPTER 4

On the last day, the weather still wasn't good. The Navy helicopter took us over to the other side of the island, where most of the sea lions live. This was our last chance.

When we landed, there were plenty of sea lions and elephant seals on the beach, but the sea looked too rough for filming. While we waited for the weather to clear, we had a look around. An hour went by, but the sky was still gray, and the waves were over three feet high. Still, we decided it was now or never.

We got our gear on, and I checked my underwater cameras. My plan was to use the movie camera first. To film underwater, the movie camera has to go inside its special yellow waterproof box to keep it dry. If I got some good movie film, I would come back to the beach and get my still camera. But I was going to need a lot of luck.

Under the waves, the water was clearer than I thought it would be. We swam about, but we didn't see any sea lions.

Suddenly – whoooooosh! – the brown shape of a sea lion came rushing past. It went right up to my buddy John. He held out his stick in case he needed to push the sea lion away. He didn't need to.

Then another sea lion came rushing up to me like a fighter plane. Just at the last moment, it turned away. Then it turned and came back again. We had come searching for sea lions, but these sea lions seemed to be searching for us! I shot film as fast as I could.

CHAPTER 5

Soon, we had half a dozen sea lions racing around us. It was a little scary at first. They were so big and fast. But they didn't want to hurt us. It was like they just wanted to look at us, and to play. We were something new and different. It was an exciting experience for us too. Being with these sea lions was like watching a very special underwater dance.

They liked a game called "catch the flipper." Any flipper! Sometimes, a sea lion tried to "catch" the flipper of another sea lion by biting it gently – if the other sea lion let it! It looked just like a game of tag. They liked our flippers too!

A big bull sea lion arrived. I hoped it wouldn't turn nasty. It swam very fast, straight toward me! At the last minute it turned away, showing me all its teeth as it went past. Was it warning me, or just playing? I didn't know, but it was very big and fast … and scary.

After a while, I knew that the bull wasn't going to hurt me. It was just rough play.

A female sea lion lay on the seafloor, stirring up the sand. She stared up at me while I took her photograph. It seemed amazing that these big, wild animals were being so friendly.

They had never seen people underwater
before, but many of them had come to look
at us. I was sorry when we had to leave to be
picked up by the helicopter.

The sea lions seemed sorry too. Some of them came out of the water with us.
One seemed to be saying "Please come into the water again." It was like we had become friends – from two different worlds.

That night I felt tired but happy. It had been one of the most exciting days of my life.
I knew I had some good film and photos – and it was the first underwater film of some of the rarest sea lions in the world.

When we woke the next morning, there was a
terrific storm. The wind was lifting sheets of
water high into the air. No one could go
diving now. We had been lucky.